My jo

S Malik

My journey © 2022 S Malik

All rights reserved.

S Malik asserts the moral right to be
identified as author of this work.

Presentation by *BookLeaf Publishing*

Web: www.bookleafpub.com

E-mail: info@bookleafpub.com

ISBN: 978-93-95755-26-9

First edition 2022

Feel like in prison

There's times when he just want to leave In this
world and never come back to it,
Looking back to everything seems like he just
feel like his in prison,
There's time where he can go out and have fun,
Or times where he can go holidays and have fun,
There's alos time when he is scared to speak,
Scared to be himself
Scared being older,
Scared of meeting new people,
He so scared that he wish everything will just be
okay,
He scared if he doesn't have anyone to meet in
future noone will love him for him,
His scared of so many things and doesn't know
how to let go that fear anymore,

Creativesabz

My version of myself

This version of wasn't built overnight,
This experience and pain,
This insecurities and abuse,
This depression and a climb out of rock bottom,
I had to go through a lot of mess up things got
me where I am now,
A time come in your life when you fanily get it,
When is the midst of all fears and old hurts you
stop dead in your tracks somewhere,
The voice in your heart head you crying out,
"ENOUGH"
This moment is turning point that leads,
To success and happiness,
So today, close the door on our pass,
Open the door to our future,
Take breath step forward to a new chapter in life,
Is seem like life going do fast it is going really
fast I was 17 just the other day I now i am 19
turning 20 sometimes feels like 16 again,
Now is new chapter and new beginning of new
life,
Is been 5 years sinces I worte poems since I was
16 now I am 20 time does really fly is like I was
16 other day and I worte my poems,

TIMES FLYS

Creativesabz

Waiting for you

My heart was writing for you,
Every lesson I was learning,
Every heartbreak I was earning,
Was cracking me open,
Making me true,
If I olny I knew,
My heart was yawning for you,
And waiting for me,
To learn what I need to know,
And go where I need to go,
To make me who I am today,
Then it was olny matter of time,
Till thus universe made you mine,
And my heart felt it may burst in tears when I
first met you,
What a beautiful sight,
To what it is timing is right,
You are one great preson I have known,
Your most kindest understanding preson I know,
You make me who I am,
You make know I am beautiful,
The reason why I love you is because you don't
care about anything but me and you are so

amazing when you give me comments and make
so good about myself,
I love you to the moon and back sometimes I
feel like if wish we had a future together

Creativesabz

Tommrow is another day

Not mabye , not tommrow,
Not someday,
Right now at this very moment,
I realized something I need you,
I trust you,
I admire you,
I want you,
You can be worng,
A lot of time,
& we can fight,
& get mad at each other,
But nothing,
Nothing Is this world know that fact is I love
you,
I love you always
You always on mind can't stop thinking about
you ,
You make my day I can't believe I met u

Creativesabz

Love

When I was young I thought i knew everything
mabye thought I knew what love was once upon
time,
As I got older I realise I there so much I don't
know,
Then thought lobe will be powerful in the world
I was worng,
If threw force between love they was timing but
who know manye I find my true love soon
(inshallah)

Creativesabz

Promises

You lied, I cried,
You left, I hurt,
You forgot, I remember,
You promised, I kept it,
You're done, I was trying,
You love me,
Stop lying,
All of these lies I feel make me re-rhink
Realty and how most of my life I spend my life
with you just a lie and how a haunting memory,
I hoped you'd be my last you changed really fast,
All we had, turned into dust, as my heart slowly
turns into rust

Creativesabz

His afraid

He so scared nobody will love him anymore,
His scared how his future will be like,
More then ever his scared of many things that
could effect himself,
His scared of darkness,
His of light,
There's time where his think his doing the right
things but then the right things he does seem to
be worng,
Sometimes his does know what is right or
worng,
Is like say in one blind of eye everything
changes for example growing up, your age and
who you become as person everything change
from that nothing easy everything becomes Hard
as you older,
The most things his afraid is that what if nobody
love him ever or what if nobody love me at all

Creativesabz

She doesn't want be that girl anymore

She hate being kind,
She hate being friendly,
She hate when people comment saying she
people bestie because she is caring and kind girl
who is friendly always ask people how they are,
Then next day people will say oh your you are
they bestie because you talk them everyday,
Or people will say oh you are they best friends
because I am always kind and friendly and
Always I regret being that girl,
She just want to change her presonality more she
want to be a rude girl and n bad girl she doesn't
want to be known as that friendly kind caring
girl anymore she want people to hate
her.

Creativesabz

Sometimes

Sometimes I feel like I am not good enough,
Is like one day u feel so pretty then next day you
feels like not pretty enough,
There's part of me think deeply into my future
thinking what will happened because I don't
have a good life well I do but not I school wise
just family wise,
Sometimes there's part of me that is lonely and
sometimes I feel trapped like nones round me,
Then I realise I have alot people by my side
eveyday who support me all time,
I know there's always up n downs with family,
But some how u grew alot of happiness with
them if you try to get along with them

Creativesabz

Memories

There's moments I think about you everyday,
I feel like everytime I miss the moments and
memories we had together,
I try to forgot the memories we had trying to get
out my head,
But is impossible to remove the feeling I had for
you Icl u still have feelings for you,
The Introduction to my life
Everybody left, that's the story of my life
Unappreciated even when I'm in disguise
Unappreciated even when I do provide,
Is just I feel empty without you,
I can't lose my feelings for you,
We had our memories together that go away
because is always in my head

Creativesabz

Left me

They left me hurt and lonely and it hurt but I feel
better now,
I feel broken but everything seem like we had to
be part way from everything,
Our love has been broken now there no turn
around,
in that moment, all things beautiful and bright
seemed to disappear. When he left so did the
beauty and good in the world,
he let go. Like a feather in the wind, his soul
flew lightly in the current of death, calm and
peaceful. Up and down he went, until he landed
in the river and he realise he going through
phase,
and in that moment, my heart dropped as my
fear of losing you was coming true.
and in that moment,
he realized,
he was better off alone,
sitting in the dark where no one can hurt her,
like he had,
And the preosn love won't be part my life
because love is always complicated and love just
broken,

Sometimes I wish you was part of my life
everyday I cry thinking about you,

Creativesabz

Dyslexia

Dyslexia is not disability,
It is a way to learn new things,
Writing, speaking, reading, remembering
number's,
Dyslexia is not illness is just hard to learn to
certain situations such as in exam and in class,
You can forgot your time table and remember it
if you Keep practicing,
Don't give up in yourself try you best that all it
matters

Creativesabz

Open your eyes

Open your eyes to the beauty around you,
Open you mind to the wonders of life,
Open you heart to those who love you,
And always be true to yourself,
Never be ashamed of scars,
You were stronger then whatever tried to hurt
you,
The Open eyes of a wolf speak mysteries of life,
We must want to listen from our hearts,
To hear what they says,
When it hurts to looks back,
and you scared to look ahead,
You can look beside you and always remember
that,
You have Allah (swt) by your side,
Not matter how badly people treat you,
Never drop down to their level,
Just know you are better and walk away from
them as long as you know doing right then
everything is better for you,
The most things is focus on you and Allah (stw)
he has our hearts we have his two,

Creativesabz

Inspired

When it come to my writing I get inspired by
anything and everything,
People having faith in you,
People saying you got this,
People who believe in you,
People who know you can do things with trying
your best and not giving up ,
These people are the people you want get
inspired by,
Like I said in my recent peom my cousins
inspired me she got me into writing my own
poems,
Anyone can inspired it's don't have to be a
family member it can be who ever you want it to
me,
Try know that if you believe yourself then other
people will belive in you,
Also if other people know you can do it then you
know you can do it to,

Creativesabz

Oh Allah

Oh Allah,
I wish that everyone could see,
How your love has set me free,
and made me storng,
Ya Allah keep me focused on my purpose,
If Allah (swt) has written something to be yours,
It will be,
Time might not be different,
The journey might be different,
But it will be yours,
Allah (swt) will always bring to you what you're
meant to hear and see,
Don't worry people's true colours will always
comes out in the end,
Just keep your heart clean and pure towards all,
Even if you are in darkness side Allah (swt)
Has neve left you,
He never leave you behind
Always trust him,
Trust your lord with your heart,
He will always understanding it,

Creativesabz

No sleep

There's moments where I am so confused
and lost sometimes I just want to sleep forever
and forgot about all these pain,
I am okay
But I am not happy or sad
Most of time I don't want I am is just mix
emotions all of again,
The feelings when you not necessarily sad but
you feel so empty ,
There's people out there who want to get to
know you but still want to stab u in back and
give the balme to you sometime u feel like why
you dealing with so many fake people in your
life,
Is like saying I don't who I am then you wait I
know who I am now as day go by you realise
you really don't who you are anymore like you
find out who you are but the you end up in the
worng path,
Sometimes I wonder what is like to wake up and
love yourself,
To look at the mirror And not want to cry,
Not feel ugly but feel pretty,

Sometimes you feel like you not good enough
and you just feel trapped,
Hiding my tears in rain,
Walking in shadow is another type of pain,
Feels dead when adrenaline drain,
Still smiling at mirrors,
No more running from ny fears,

Creativesabz

With you

When you feel down, alone, demotivated:
Pray, prayer is solution to all you problems,
Remember Allah (swt) he always remember
you,
He is the most forgiven,
Most kind,
He will never stop forgiven you,
If your sins were reach to the sky and you turned
back asked
'Ya Rab , please forgive me,
He forgive you,
You are his most loved creation,
Know that when you are alone,
He always with you

Creativesabz

Lost

I am lost once again,
Who I am with all my creation,
I used to neve trust Allah (stw) plans,
And used think my world wasn't meant to be,
Now I trust Allah (swt) more then anything,
I know it's meant to be,
I say hand is shaking but my heart is breaking
with tears in my eye I hurt alot,
I thought my life is not easy but as time, day
months and even year pass by
You realise you have respect for your lord more
then anything,
You ask for help you will know his near

Creativesabz

Inspiration

I never thought I will be writing my own poems,
until there was a cousins of mine who inspired
me how to write my own poetry,
Every since she started to write poems I was like
to myself I want to learn how to write my own
poems,
I started to write and write to see if I was any
good,
I kept writing my owns one,
My cousins like or don't matter about the
spelling, it matter about if you know what you
talking about then is fine,
Every since then I started to write my own
poems but it wasn't very good,
Reading her poems has inspired me alot,
When I was 10 she was like my inspiration still
since this day she still is my inspiration
I wouldn't be writing my own poems if I didn't
have this amazing cousin in my life,

Creativesabz

Voice in my head

As I walk down the street I heard voice in my head,
Is like I hear people calling my name,
I hear all the loves one voices in ny head then I slowly close my eyes and I realise is just my imagination, I put my ear phone to listen to music I still hear voices in my head and aloud then I take one ear phone of I realise Is still my imagination and now days I have no conversations in my head then real life,
I am crying and screaming when he love ones voice is my head,
But I realise is just my imagination or a dream

Creativesabz

I am okay

They asking u how you doing?
I reply: I am okay,
But I am not really okay,
They ask you how are you?
I reply: I am okay,
But I am not really okay,
I say I am okay, But I am not okay,
I am not happy nor I am sad,
I just simply confused,
I Don't know why,
and I am sorry,
I say I am okay and pretend to be okay when in
reality I am not okay,
You whisper into my ears asking me,
Are you okay,
I say, yeah I am okay,
When really...
I'm not okay.

Creativesabz